A Map Towards Fluency

LISA KELLY is half-Danish and half-deaf. She is the Chair of *Magma Poetry* and co-edited issue 63, *The Conversation Issue*; and issue 69, *The Deaf Issue*. She is a regular host of poetry evenings at the Torriano Meeting House, London, and has an MA in Creative Writing with Distinction from Lancaster University. Her pamphlets are *Bloodhound* (Hearing Eye, 2102) and *Philip Levine's Good Ear* (Stonewood Press, 2018).

She is currently a freelance journalist specialising in technology, and has worked as an actress, life model, Consumer Champion, waitress, sales assistant and envelope stuffer. She teaches creative writing and poetry in performance at the Torriano Meeting House.

T0158639

LISA KELLY

A Map

Towards Fluency

CARCANET

This book is for my family: past and present

First published in Great Britain in 2019 by
Carcanet
Alliance House, 30 Cross Street
Manchester M2 7AQ
www.carcanet.co.uk

A CIP catalogue record for this book is
available from the British Library.
ISBN 978 1 78410 711 6

Book design by Andrew Latimer
Printed in Great Britain by SRP Ltd, Exeter, Devon

The publisher acknowledges financial
assistance from Arts Council England.

Contents

VII. NEATLINE

A Map Towards Fluency

I.

Scale and Accuracy

Whitewash

The faded Swastika on the side of the barn
is showing through the latest layer of paint
and must be painted over by the owner again.

Our generation is generous it seems.
Over dinner we discuss how the farmer's daughter
was a victim of her beautiful genes,

no choice but to take the Nazi officer's seed.
What would you do? The sort of moral dilemma
sorted over a second bottle, until resentment breeds.

Your great uncle *a prêté serment* –
swore an oath to Pétain – and was *préfet*
of Calvados. I translate this to an easy life in Caen.

I ask if, after the war, he was detained.
You say, *surveillance gardée*, (is there a difference?)
but his possessions and farm were returned.

I boast of my Danish uncle who fought in the resistance.
You stress yours was an uncle *only* by marriage.
Where is this going? Nowhere, but we are persistent,

stripping off layers of skin to expose raw nerves,
find iron in blood, the cross in the rib cage –
what of us that shows through, what it proves.

Bureau Mazarin

It stands like a tragedy
Strikingly teased data

Apart from its creator
A rip at comforter's art

Walnut, olive-wood, brass
A wad blows revolutions

We are shabby observers
Everywhere basso barbs

To this noble narrator
Betrothals rain on rot

The mob would have
Behaved owl mouth

Broken and burnt it
Drunken ribbon tat

Or used it in the kitchen
Kinesthetic oh red unit

The legs were broken
Berserk genteel who

And the locks were forced
Weathercocks end or fled

Left in the attic
Theft intact lie

Furniture restorer
Retrofit rerun ruse

Restores
Or resets

Late seventeenth century
Evanescent they lute rent

Your pretty legs
Surgery yet plot

Their pitilessness
Litheness its spire

The cheap Kandinsky print
Hyphenated pranks ink tic

Gallops away in embarrassment
Rams a man powerlessly abating

Aubade for an Artist

Of course, the morning came; it always does,
but before was an evening, and it was
such an evening I felt already afraid
of morning before the light began to fade.

He cooked while I looked out of a sash window.
As he set the table, I said, *There's a rainbow*,
and he replied, *I painted the sky for you.*
Such a perfect response: too good to be true.

So we ate, and I remember it was fish,
which I don't much like, but again the dish
of tarnished silver was so perfectly placed
on a crushed red velvet curtain, draped

over a folding table in the room's centre
that the flavour meant less than the gesture,
the blunt edge, notched tip of a fish knife –
I thought, *Can we possibly still our lives.*

Of course, the morning came; it always does,
but before was an evening, and it was
such an evening I felt already afraid
of morning before the light began to fade.

Life Model

I can't look him in the eye because I'm naked.
And I can't look down because he's naked.
So I look at the circle of people, who aren't naked,
but are nakedly impatient
for me to take my place on the podium,
so they can cover their naked canvasses with charcoal.

My back is skin-to-skin with his back;
there's not a cigarette paper between us,
and I curl my legs around myself
to try and look like the statue of the Little Mermaid
and create interesting contours,
and stare out, motionless, at the sea of blank faces.

And I hope I don't sneeze.
And I hope I don't sweat.
And I hope I don't secrete.
Because I'm fish naked.
And there's no-one to mop me up.
And there's no-one to dab me down.

And this is what it feels like to cease to exist,
to be naked and have no-one ask,
Are you ok?
to have no-one say anything,
to have a partner who lies against you naked
and doesn't care what you think, or feel,
who doesn't know you, or want to know you.

Four hours later, clothed, and £16 cash-in-hand richer,
I leave to meet my artist boyfriend, in the gallery
with naked canvasses on the walls, and guinea pigs,
like little muffs, running around the floor,
dodging boots and heels, stopping to nibble carrots,
and snuggling down in beds of pubic straw.

And I think, maybe I'm an artist,
or at least a crucial part of the artistic process,
like a naked canvas, or a mermaid, or a guinea pig.

Maybe I do exist.

And maybe one day there will be a picture of me in an attic,
which will stay young forever, and I feel so confident,
I answer the exhibitor's question, *What do you do?*
with, *I'm a life model.*

And he replies, *You're a stripper.*
You strip off for £4 an hour.
You're nothing but a strip artist.
And my boyfriend, who's in our group, says nothing.
His face is a blank canvas.

And this is what it feels like to cease to exist,
to feel naked and have no-one ask,
Are you ok?
to have no-one say anything,
to have a partner who lies against you naked
and doesn't care what you think, or feel,
who doesn't know you, or want to know you.

And at that moment, I decide to exist, and I say,
You're nothing but a ripoff artist,
dressed in the Emperor's new clothes.

And I don't feel naked.
I feel like I'm wearing steel-capped boots,
and a breastplate, and a leather jacket with studs.
I feel like I'm wearing the Arc de Triomphe as a knuckle duster,
and the Statue of Liberty as headgear.

And I think, forget trying to look like a statue of the Little Mermaid,
and forget not sneezing, or sweating or secreting,
and forget the blank canvasses on the walls, and the blank faces,
and forget staying young in an attic, and totally forget the guinea pigs.

And forget having a partner who lies against you naked
and doesn't care what you think, or feel,
who doesn't know you, or want to know you.

Slant of Summer

There's a black and white photo of my half-siblings
stuck in my memory, their legs in wooden stocks.
My sister's head is tilted. She is half-smiling.
The white bow in her hair matches her white dress,
although what is white could be pink or powder green
in that slant of summer. Our brother, laid-back,
leans away from the lens. This is his time to dream,
fringe falling over one eye, on half-term break
from boarding school, where he was force-fed maggots
and sat half-asleep to warm the toilet seat
for a prick of a prefect, and there's a cuteness-
cum-cockiness in his eye which might or might not
antagonise the man who will cuckold his father –
who may or may not already be part of the picture.

Six Perspectives on Lilian Kjærulff

2 April 1934 – 17 July 2010

i. *second daughter from second marriage*

I know why you married so young.
You curtsied to him, offered your gloved hand
with your girlish good manners,
straight off the Esbjerg boat.
Your signature move: that dip.
You were a tall girl; your mother warmed
to see another top you by an inch.
You told me once, if out together,
you walked in the gutter,
so she didn't feel so small. Nothing
bitchy meant by her remark,
Se, en anden giraf!
That's why curtseying came so naturally:
maternal inculcation. Of course,
when you made yourself small for him,
he had to fall in love; and you were trained to please.

ii. *first husband*

It wasn't the height gap; it was the age gap
that bothered me: 13 years, I grey, you blonde.
Your accent I found charming,
Wheel for dinner darling?
but then tiring. I was a golfer, not a teacher.
I liked your sportiness. Your height must have helped:
Danish Junior Tennis Champion at 15.
Imagine. You at full stretch

smashing a ball, your dress rising.
When we met, you dropped a bunch of marguerites,
(well, that's what we told the children)
bent at the same time, bumped heads,
and hearts.
You told me 13 was a lucky number in Denmark.
Sod the age gap:
I wanted you.

iii. best friend

I called you Great Dane; you called me She.
Both with two children, both golf widows,
both with frightful mothers-in-law –
yours called you The Hun.
Bound to become friends darling.
Of course I knew. Everything.
You covered for me, I covered for you.
Friends do that. I often brought
my lover to lunch. You served
champagne and Smörgåsbord.
There was that time
you said Dickie tried to kiss you,
but he liked to tickle a lady
with his moustache. Just his way.
Nothing meant by it. All fun and games.
We got over it. Great Dane, such a sport!

iv. second husband

Other men's wives:
neglected, grateful for attention,
but most importantly no bother.
You were different.
He was a drinking pal at the club.
We had handicaps in common,
not much else. Until you.
I want another drink.
Will you dance with my wife?
Of course, I obliged.
The club tolerated affairs,
but it treated divorcees
like the Irish. We had to move.
I never regretted anything.
You were my Lil.
Jeg elsker dig.

v. first daughter from first marriage

I was 11; it was a bit of an adventure packing.
I knew you were unhappy,
the last two years sleeping in my room,
making yourself small to fit in the bed,
long summers in Copenghagen.
You left dad a Dear John note.
I understood, but I loved him.
The adventure was soon over:
I missed school, my friends, London.
Buckinghamshire was just leafy. I went home.
He married the barmaid at the club;
she was nice until she took his name.

You phoned him once to tell him
to tell her to stop.
He said, *If you hadn't left*
we wouldn't be having this conversation.

vi. mother

You were my only child.
And you left.
I saw you just two weeks every year:
in one house, and then another. Imagine.
Four grandchildren I couldn't speak to.
I'm not trying to make you feel guilty,
but imagine. You broke my heart.
You could have had anyone, a Danish
anyone. I'm not trying to make you feel
guilty, but imagine what it was like
when I became ill. Your father on his own.
My memory going, repeating myself over
and over. I was so proud of you.
I want you to know that. Imagine how proud:
a champion at 15, beautiful manners.
And so tall.

A&E

If this waiting is hellish, then the sick are limbo dancing;
only those who are bent double, or on the floor, puddles
of their former selves, have a hope of getting under the bar,
progressively lowered as more contorted squeeze through.

If the woman in a white coat is god, then the boy with bleeding hands
has stigmata, the man with closed eyes on the stretcher is Lazarus,
and the toddler pushing donkey-on-wheels up and down,
up and down, is one of the Four Horsemen of the Apocalypse.

If this is a place of worship, then the grey kidney-shaped receptacles
are donation plates passed around for contributions from the faithful,
hopeful they are worthy of saving. If this is where you think the wait
will end within four hours, then think again, the end is always waiting.

Death Certificate, Burnt Oak

Dealing with the paperwork of dying,
the registrar looks dead bored, and, sighing,
he asks for my dad's place and date of death
and birth, job, names, and last usual address.
As he writes it down, his signet ring gleams
on his little finger. He looks up, leans
towards my mother, and his pen is poised,
as he asks her, as wife of the deceased,
her name, and, at last, her occupation.
Housewife, she says. A hesitation,
he wrinkles his brow, and, again, he sighs,
taps his pen, *Is that all? Yes,* she replies,
and in her voice, there's no hint of recoil,
while I said nothing, but boiled. And still boil.

The Shadow Cast

'I'm not casting the human figure,
but the shadow that is cast.'
— Alberto Giacometti

I did not sit in the car
watching the nervous grass,
the bush in full swell,
waiting for it to crash
into the windscreen.
I put down the book
with its blank white cover,
took off silver sandals,
placed dark glasses in the
cup holder, opened
the resistant door,
ran at full pelt across
the field. I did not flinch
when a nasty, little stone
chipped off the road,
burrowed into my sole.

I did not discard shorts
on the shore, tear off top,
revealing goosed flesh
in bra and pants, did not think
how my mother would never
have behaved like this,
would sit in her deckchair
windcheatered, headscarfed,
in sensible sandals,
watching nervous
Giacometti figures wading out
at ridiculous angles

to the Atlantic crests
arms flailing in a last-ditch
attempt to wave her in
to join the undeniable fun.
I did not resent,
succumbing to a
grey-blue wave
the colour of our lips later,
that she never came in
as she towelled us hard
to rough up blood.

I did not smack
into the surf, scream
as it took me and my knickers
down. I did not cut my wrist
on a nasty little stone, swallow
salt, choke, stand up
to my children's laughter
at my demi-nakedness,
pull up pants full of shale.
I did not think, *At least I'm fun*,
did not wrestle with a khaki-coat
briefly turned kite
casting a shadow on the sand,
before I could zip myself in,
and wait huddled on a rock.
I did not say,
Can I go back to the car?

Ø

Danish for island
a new word
new world
to explore

My tongue
tastes the sound of Ø
touches its shores
its limits

I dream of Ø, wishing
it in my blood
as the English sound
that comes so easily, it is thoughtless

Ø floats
like those white blood cells
that gave my mother
& her tongue life

My mouth has a Caliban look
monsterish in expressiveness
and more ridiculously
round than Ø

Surrounded by a sea of white
Ø is what it means
but I can't possess
even this small word

The axis cutting
north-east to south-west
makes Ø
a *No Entry* sign

I will navigate Ø
the line going through
is a river perhaps
and will lead to fresh water

II.

Coordinates

This Is Not a Road Trip

Today, the day I learn Patrick Minaud is dead,
      a boy picks up a stone and hurls it into the sea,
           as if he is angry with the sea,
      as if he wants to show the sea what he can do.
There is no eternal note, just a plop.

I do not know the boy beyond being dark-haired,
      defiant. Go boy!
           Go throw another stone into the sea.
      Today, the day a boy hurls a stone into the sea,
the tide is out in the bay, as if the sea has learnt its lesson to obey.

A horse and rider are in the middle of the bay
      as if they could, in time,
           walk on water.
      And the dark, wet sand is a salve to the horse's hooves,
as the rhythm of the horse is a salve to the rider.

Minaud's house overlooks the bay,
      boundaries fortified by granite boulders.
           And the boulders sit hard on the pale, dry sand
      for they will never succumb to the sea. Far out at sea,
an old man rows for shore with pregnant nets, waiting to spill silver.

And there will always be an old man rowing for shore
      with pregnant nets, waiting to spill silver.
           And a horse and rider will always be in the middle of the bay,
      almost able to walk on water.
And a boy will always be hurling a stone into the sea.

And the sea, having learned its lesson,
    will always be in retreat,
        scared of the boulders
    guarding Minaud's land
which will never blow hither and thither like the pale, dry sand.

A Desultory Day

It's the sort of day with spit but no polish,
the sort of day when a neighbour makes hay
with my husband's amiable manner
and extracts a maybe to sort out her fruit trees.
It's the sort of day you say, *It's that sort of day*
to help you get through. It's the sort of day
I fall in love with a Japanese man
for the way he stands magnificently
in his trunks while his daughters play croquet.
It's the sort of day a towel serves
as a skirt, and a jumper as a headscarf,
the sort of day eyes jump from horse rider
to horse rider in the bay. It's the sort of day
a father drags a pram across the sand backwards,
the sort of day a fat baby tries to catch
fat feet, the sort of day when not just thoughts stray.

Trailing Spouse

Near the pool, I picked a frangipani blossom.
By the time I spoke to the maid, its petal edges
were breakfast cereal brown.

Everything is either overripe or sticky –
mangoes, rice, my thighs. Except the maid.
A silk dress would slip and pool at her ankles.

Like the pomeranian, the baby must be paraded
every day at least twice on the little patch
of grass with all the other babies and pomeranians.

Work. The Mall. Both are air-conditioned.
Both colonise time. There are compensations,
but like the breeze, they are mostly offshore.

Battling for their place under the ceiling light,
the moths are migraine-inducing. We drink
imported wine. She doesn't want sex.

Wavering

Winding back from the last tube,
  I see a girl on the kerb,
in open-toed heels, poured
  into an off-white dress in this cold,
leaning into an open window, drunk,
  pouring her heart out, and as I pass
I hear the policeman,
  from the squat comfort of his seat
shout, *Carry on like that,*
  you'll be in the back of my van,
so I stop, turn and think
  whether I should go up to her,
calm her down, ask him to lay off,
  but instead I stand there, tipsy
from the half bottle of wine,
  a by-stander - and in that pause,
the girl is joined by another girl,
  who screams at the policeman: suddenly
police cars are pulling up, sirens
  screaming, police spill out,
dressed in thick uniforms, not stumbling,
  just purposefully herding
girls into the back of the van,
  which speeds off – the police
get back into their cars, slam doors,
  rev up, drive off, and there is nothing
more to do except go home,
  wonder what might have happened
if I'd protested soberly, directly.

Corona/Cuts

after John Donne

They search my bag like an abandoned flat,
raking for answers to unformed questions,
fumbling with tissues and bits of old tat,
unable to grasp haptic impressions.
What do I know of my son's compass point?
Why did this prick try to hide in the seams?
Have they not heard we all have a fixed foot,
how the other hearkens after, and leans?
My circle is just. My son is secure.
Absence expansion in a foreign land.
Sharp reminders and tokens underscore
each search a charade, til steel is in hand.
Let us close this bag and let me go through.
This flat is unoccupied, the rent due.

This flat is unoccupied, the rent due.
We salvage the mattress from Spain's dark street.
Erect steel bars for a four-poster view,
lie on the bloodstain covered by a sheet.
From here, we hear the bells of Aranjuez,
sad chimes from Rodrigo's Concierto.
Since thou and I sigh one another's breath,
engrave, *Antes muerto que mudado.*
Our sons will not dare into Walthamstow,
Battersea, Harlesden, Oakwood, Marylebone.
They will not venture into Enfield, Bow,
Wandsworth, Peckham Rye, Uxbridge, Mile End, home.
Let us close this flat. Rodrigo is owed.
Sooner dead than changed, but seeds must be sowed.

Sooner dead than changed, but seeds must be sowed.
Who can stop him winding down the wrong path?
At the round earth's imagin'd corners blow
nose, wipe streaming eyes, repair your torn half.
He strayed outside his postcode, and was lost.
The subway where he might play his last scene.
No time even to be idle. The cost
of the cut through, alley, underpass, green.
All whom war, death, age, agues, tyrannies,
despair, law, chance, being in the wrong ends hath slain,
to your scatter'd bodies go. Authorities,
politicians search solutions in vain;
can't contain measure. The globes four corners
a dream. Sons walk the next street, foreigners.

A dream, sons walk the next street, foreigners
share conversation, customs, cares, break bread,
An Europe, Afric, and an Asia blurs
into one round ball. Dream that no-one bled.
Dream the difference between butterfly
and butter as descriptions for a knife.
Dream the stand-off, after-math pass you by,
dream you applied pressure to save a life.
His dream of diverse shores is a nightmare,
our sons reject the Seven Sleepers' den.
One little room is not an everywhere,
a dream of safety, his wool-lined pen.
Not thy sheep, thine image, servant. Thy son.
Wake, and batter your heart, *What have I done?*

Wake, and batter your heart, *What have I done?*
He stole a knife from the cutlery drawer.
What reason? In their own words, here are some:
To protect myself against my father.
My dad was stabbed to death when I was three.
I will stab them first. It's for protection.
They would have beaten the shit out of me.
It is a tool for intimidation.
It does not matter how tough the laws are.
The risk that someone will pull one on you.
I would, if anyone took things too far.
People are always tooled up; it's not new.
Thank God. Chopped, had I not had it with me.
Angels affect us oft, and worshipp'd be.

Angels affect us oft, and wordshipp'd be.
Knife Angel is hoisted by cranes to sky.
Society looks up and strains to see.
Here is a glint that is not in the eye,
not in a voice, not in a shapeless flame –
one hundred thousand confiscated blades,
messages engraved on wings, victims' names.
This monument, an iron-monger's trade.
As yet but knock, breathe, shine and seek to mend
Your force to break, blow, burn, and make me new.
Mettle tested so we can comprehend
weight of wasted lives, hope forged anew.
Stamp your mark. Stamp out this epidemic.
Each loss named, a wound. Each cut, systemic.

Each loss named, a wound. Each cut, systemic.
Handle, point, edge, grind, blade, spine, fuller, guard,
escutcheon, bevel, gut-hook, choil, crock stick
ricasso, bolster, hilt, tang, butt, lanyard.
Athame, Balisong, Cane, Deba bōchō,
Ear, Facón, Gravity, Hunting, Izar,
Janbiya, Kukri, Laguiole, Mandau,
Navaja, Opinel, Pata, Qama,
Rondel, Shiv, Trench, Urumi, Voulge, Wedung
X-Acto, Yoroi-dōshi, Zombie Knives.
Mother, Father, Sister, Brother, Daughter, Son.
Friend, Lover, Neighbour, Society, Lives.
Stab, shank, chib, zoor, jook, slice, wet steel. For what?
They search my bag like an abandoned flat.

III.

Orientation

Out of Order

You say a sign should hang from my ear,
you say torture with Chinese Whispers,
like the door on the toilet refusing to flush.
I'll say whatever comes into my ear as shush.
I say there is no blockage, no glue or wax,
you'll accuse me of negative feedback,
just nerves dead as disconnected wires.
I say thank God for books, my ear retires,
you say playing with a rotary phone
far from the playground's monotone,
picking up the receiver to my good ear,
you say you'll get me in the mere –
bad: dial tone/no dial tone, is wacko.
Oh-noes playing Marco Polo,
I say I'm testing how to differentiate
a unilateral ear unable to locate
between fitting in/not fitting in.
Oi! Are you deaf or something?

Philip Levine's Good Ear

Your poem, 'Nightship' starts with '*Ceuta*', how you say you'd like to go there.
I'm not sure how to pronounce Ceuta, but say Kway-t<u>a</u>, not having been there,
and not knowing how to approach a strange Spanish word with my stupid tongue.
If someone could sound it out slow and sure, I would not necessarily remember.
I know this, because someone did, and I don't. It's in my head, you say it, Say-uu-t<u>a</u>
or maybe Sew-t<u>a</u>. Sounds come and go, some dock, and some like your ship, sail on.
In your poem, the ticket seller's clock is stuck at quarter-to-three, and of course
clock rhymes with *dock*, but there are no clues about what might rhyme with Ceuta,
although this would not help with the back-of-the-throat v. tongue/teeth approach
to the opening syllable, and is not something to get hung up on. Your thought,
Africa, a whole new world! is probably a key moment for many readers,
but apart from the fear of stumbling over Ceuta my interest is in what you hear –
the three layers of sound: water crashing into the hull & beneath that the steady
beating of the engine & beneath that the wind whispering '*Ceuta*' into your *good ear*.
This is what I leave with from your poem – your sensitivity to timbres of sound
and a shared good ear. My deaf ear says Kway-t<u>a</u>, my good ear says if the wind whispers,
then it must be Say-uu-t<u>a</u> or Sew-t<u>a</u>. Your last line gives away nothing: *Starless, the sky gave
away nothing.*

Herring Loss

Half heard, now half remembered
what was it I thought you said
as I beg my brain for the word I know
begins with *b*? The sense of something
on the tip of my tongue, which lurks
behind bottom teeth as lips purse *b*
goldfishing empty speech bubbles.

The Christmas cracker joke you told,
*What did the fish say when he swam
into a wall?* has an in-built sinker,
if not the right line, hooking *codswallop*,
all manner of red herrings, as I bang
my head against a brick wall, and hit
upon it was not *b* but *d. Damn!*

Lady Monoaural

after Elizabeth Bishop's 'The Gentleman of Shalott'

Half is enough,
she wishes to be quoted as saying at present:
that sense of constant re-adjustment
she loves, finds exhilarating
the uncertainty –
and her ear can clasp
another sound.
She can talk and run rings around
while a mouth stays put,
only one ear, etc.
she's in a fix –
if the mouth slips
but to such economical design
she's resigned.

Thought, she thinks, might be affected,
and if half her ear's refracted,
but there's no proof, either.
There's little margin for error.
A mirror image,
but as to which side is in or out,
she's in no doubt.
Down the edge, or rather
down her middle
the impasse must stretch.
For why should she be doubted,
half-hearing lass
her person was
she felt in modesty.

Of what we realign,
somewhere along the line
of a mithered reflection,
it's the indication
to her mind.
Ear and so on,
of good ear and deaf ear and
in this arrangement
nor hears a stranger
nor the other,
nor a different holler
for neither is clearer.
Next the mirror,
which ear lies?
Which ear's her ear?

Best Seat in the House

my deafness	trumps	your male ego
your male ego	trumps	my television programme
my television programme	trumps	Made in Chelsea
Made in Chelsea	trumps	slobbing out
slobbing out	trumps	scoffing a family-sized bar
scoffing a family-sized bar	trumps	hiding family-sized bar
hiding a family-sized bar	trumps	tearing up cushions
tearing up cushions	trumps	screaming and shouting
screaming and shouting	trumps	my deafness

Blotted Copybook

BLOT   BLOT   BLOT   BLOT

BLOT   BLOT   BLOT   BLOT

BLOT   BLOT   BLOT   BLOT

BLOT   BLOT   BLOT   BOLT

A Map Towards Fluency

i. Bedrock

I map *a*---to my left thumb

Alex maps *a*---------------------------------------to his right thumb

e-- to my left forefinger

poor Alex, the teacher can't map sinistral----------------------to dextral
thesaurus maps sinistral--to sinister
a hammer mapped a red line-------------------- to his drummer's hand

i-- to my left middle finger
(Sophie maps *i*----------------------------------- to her *swear finger*)

o---to the gold of my ring finger
u-- to my left pinkie

map a twist of fist in the gut--to hate
a raised pinkie thrust forward------------------------------------to bad
an open palm on the heart--to like

finger men meet-- to greet

hands beckon a welcome---------------------------------- at waist level
the weight of weather----------------------- at the altitude of cheekbones

Helena, who can't remember the palm-to-palm swish of her capital *H*
marks each digit with a marker pen----------------------------------*a*
--*e*
--*i*
--*o*
--*u*

(is this cheating?)

ii. Deposition of Sediment

Words are shifting animals
                        a fish is a handshimmer
a cat is claws, preening whiskers   a bird, a forefinger beaking a thumb

Colours clothe the body in a flash of flesh

Red *brushes* lips   Blue *strokes* back of hand
Green *grazes* forearm   Black *knuckles* cheek
Pink *taps* nose   White   *flares*   fingers

What has happened to Alex?
                        Helena has changed her shift, and is here
Late from an audition, Sophie circles sorry at the centre of her chest, her cheeks
a tapped nose

We bring our colours and animals with us

        Helena, a forefinger beaking thumb, settles on the edge of her chair
        Alex, an absent handshimmer

iii. Outcrop

Jean
our teacher
is a landmark
All eyes look to her
What can you see out of your
peripheral vision? Furrows forming
and reforming on ever-more familiar faces
Gestures formed and reformed by ever-more
familiar hands: rings, scars, tattoos. We keep our
distance. Eyes cannot whisper. Air, larynx, tongue:
all fingers and thumbs. As a child, Jean was forced to
sit on her hands. *Don't point! Don't touch!* Now her hands
guide us towards an alternative view. She signs, we are touched

iv. Precious Minerals

Context is everything

We are unearthing

the philosopher's stone

Base metal can be turned into   a fist
on a fist
flexing into splayed fingers

Bank is   a fist with thumb cocked, stamping the palm
Aid is   a fist with thumb up, proffered on the palm

How old?   fingers dance on the nose
How much?   fingers dance on the chin

Alex is in   a heavy metal band

On a world tour without him, it is laughing all the way to
                  the fist with thumb cocked, stamping the palm

Helena's fingers dance on her chin

On a world tour without him, it cannot offer
                  a fist with thumb up, proffered on the palm

Alex says he is feeling his age

Sophie's fingers dance on her nose

v. Erosion

I imagine our hands chopped off as Philomela had her tongue cut out
What would there be to say? How would we say it?
Not able to weave our stories into a tapestry
Alex unable to drum his rhythm. Sophie
unable to sign her song. Helena
unable to recall her felt-tipped
fingers. Alex laughs, which
is how it should be
We are going our
separate ways
towards fluency
and erosion
The future
a hand thrust
forward
the past
a wave
over the
shoulder

IV.

Projection

÷

This is our event horizon, the sun a black dot
ogling its reflection in the ocean of it all,

the line one of us crossed, obol on tongue,
the other an observer light cannot reach,

sucked in so far, returning is oblivion,
going over a spurious passage.

This is our event horizon, you horizontal,
my head hanging over yours,

a petrified intention to kiss,

the head in the golden round, divided,
each must have an eye, each a tooth.

This is our event horizon, the spot excised,
a hole stitched over, the slub in the thread

warping the line. Janus crosses the threshold,
unable to face the future, oblivious of the past.

This is our event horizon, the sun a black dot
ogling its reflection in the ocean of it all.

Polar Observations with Anagram Shadows

The moon is a hazy bitch.[1]
The underbelly of the Boeing is red.[2]
Don't say that swallow is a crossbow.[3]

A hibachi zest moth yon.
Heterogeneously hefted blind rib.
Switchboards swallow assay on tot.

---

[1] My scuffed white boots kick asphalt.
[2] My toenails are raspberry rippled.
[3] Don't say that fly is a toering gem.

Wastebaskets thickly cuff mid hoop.
Inappropriately remarry blessed.
Day fogs intermittently oh saga.

Visible Spectrum

UV-A

I'm Thea / bore three lovely children / rosy-cheeked Dawn /
rich-tressed Selene / tireless Helios whom I chase all day / holidays /
rare / just two weeks to turn golden / designer fake sunglasses /
blinded by bling / ~~Conformité Européene~~ /
UV visible spectrophotometer reveals / 23.6% UV-A light passes through /
ocular melanoma / no oracular goddess / lesson / stay out of the light /

UV-B

I'm Eos / better known as Dawn / red hair / fair skin / red lips / insatiable /
for beautiful young men / Orion / Phaeton / Kephalos / Tithonos /
some say Aphrodite's curse /some say whore / these grasshopper men /
always shrivel / must look my best / bake on a tanning bed /
no UV-B protection / skin reddening / moles raised and rosy /
in the borderlands of dark / lesson / stay out of the light /

UV-C

I'm Selene / hide my face / half hide my face / appear in a veil of silver light /
child after child / trapped in this cave / he sleeps / the eye of night /
watches / daughter after daughter / he snores / round once more /
feels like the fiftieth / remember my hair / black flowing / now my waxy skull /
on the ward / I see sisters / crescent stomachs / howling / lunatic /
UV-C light is used to sterilise / lesson / stay out of the light /

Cuddles Are Drying up Like the Sun in a Data Lake

Sun is such a hard word, like a boiled sweet
in one of those round travel sweet tins
that nobody wants unless they're sick,
those citrus colours: lemon, lime and orange
that even without tasting make your mouth water
to counter the churn in your stomach.

Sun is such a hard word, with its 's' and 'n'
that could have an 'o' or an 'i' slotted between
for that Donnian pun or a postlapsarian chime
making it harder to give birth to or acknowledge,
spat out in a sibilant spray of spittle
ending in bright, shining negation.

Sun is such a hard word, once part of Microsystems
swallowed by Oracle, its SPARC processor in LEON
designed for space use, a fully open-source
implementation that neither you nor I
can understand, the most likely meaning:
cuddles are drying up like the sun in a data lake.

Apotropaic Marks & Bodily Parts

cross your ×
sunglasses ward off the evil
/ am a sum of bodily parts

talisman or temptress, this doll
pins in her VVΛ

scratching on the windowpane, a branch
not ×

O Cathy

chthonic deities demand living VVV in sunken pots
                                  Share VVV Feast

some things are best left
unsay this broken VVΛ
cross this broken VVΛ

construct a building
                  plasterwork
                  stone, gargoyle
    *   gorgon
scribe
transcribe this broken VVΛ

Keep this VVΛ safe

tattoo your left //Λ\
ward off

Icarus, broken /
son of Daedalus

master craftsman

a horseshoe nailed above the hearth, smoke gets in your /
a horseshoe nailed above the \/\/\

lament the Labyrinth, its hexafoil [*]

Icaria

Clavicle: snaps

I

It's interesting to try and work out what I was thinking,
and the closest I get is, *How will this end?*

I'd like to think I thought profoundly as I momentarily flew,
but there was no Icarus moment, no aspiration to ascend.

2

I can't lift my arm to take off my jumper; the paramedic finds scissors,
You don't mind if I cut it off? She divests me of sodden gloves,

pulls down my wet cycling pants and helps me step into
a dry spare pair I had in my carrier. I think I've fallen in love.

3

Why do people say, *You're lucky. It could have been a lot worse.*
Why do I reply, *I was lucky. I was wearing a helmet.*

There's a bruise like an addled dandelion above my left brow,
two dents on the shell. *Yes, I was lucky. I was wearing a helmet.*

4

In the back of the ambulance, a policeman asks the paramedic
over my head, *Are her injuries life changing?*

She answers, *No,* but I imagine how someone would feel
about an overheard affirmative, a blow without warning.

5

The Collision/Incident Information form comes through the post
asking me to tick options most appropriate for *the offender*.

1) charged before a court 2) offered a Driver Improvement Course
3) warned as to driving conduct 4) take no further action 5) leave form
   on sofa.

6

I remember David Cronenberg's film *Crash* and suggest we try out
positions despite my sling, or rather because of it. I say it's about trust.

Ten minutes in, and he touches my shoulder, which is tender. Trust,
like pain, is over-rated. My right of way: the car's *thrust*.

7

Cracks in the family dynamic appear. Somehow the pieces must fit
back together, look better than good as new. The centre cannot hold

anything beyond a cup of tea, but we are learning the art of Kintsugi,
the Japanese tradition of repairing broken pots with gold.

8

I want an artist to paint the leaf on my left shoulder growing
towards my left breast – like Daphne I am turning tree,

hunted down, not by Apollo, but a Renault. At the climax,
a wooden limb, brushstrokes reveal a green mortality.

V.

Navigation

Saltatorium

O drear, O dreary dreary dirge for this deer
that hath stallèd in a ditch all anitch with fear,
and how it twitch, how it fidget and flinch
its formerly fine fetlock, fends off the dog howls,
fends off the fender of the four-by-four Ford,
fleeing its flightpath, shit trails like smoke trails
like entrails. Haven't you though, haven't you
sometimes in a sensitive somewhat sensory
rush hour of solemnity sensed its shadow?
This is no laughing matter, this is no ha-ha
wall at the Hameau de la Reine as grass grazes
garden, and your gaze graces a deer-leap into space.
This is its history, its ditch down, your disown.
Buckshot. *For 2 miles*, forever. Fallow migration.

Twenty Grains, One Scruple

'He was a contributor of poetry to various magazines.'
— New York Times, *16.10.20*

Experiments in life are a venture:
calculations of what you leave behind
tested against an immeasurable future,

but gentlemen, let us scientifically sup
on weighty matters of the soul. In my lab
fifteen dogs dying of distemper gave up

the ghost with no discernible loss of mass.
Yet friends consider: six sick patients,
all volunteers, at their lives terminus,

installed on beds placed on Fairbanks scales
sensitive to less than one-tenth of an ounce.
At the very moment a life fails

the scales dropped – not only from my eyes –
but literally by three-fourths of an ounce. Proof
the soul is material to man. As he sighs

his last breath, a hummingbird's weight
flies free; the mass of a beast with no afterlife
remains constant for it has no soul's freight

to unburden at its appointed demise.
Some have asked how did I subdue
the dogs; some answered poison. Lies.

Unlike the dogs, they thrash at truths
which they have not self-discovered.
In scrupulous experiments, like a sleuth

I eliminated factors for mortuary degravitation:
faecal matter and urine remain on the bed;
my experiments accounted for evaporation.

I, Dr Duncan MacDougall, understand dross.
I stake my reputation on what we leave behind
at death is a carcass, and a near ounce of loss.

Playing Dog

When you pass a dog, there is an option to stroke it
or kick it. The dog has an option to bite back
or roll over and offer its pink tummy to be tickled.
Which reaction is appropriate to which action
is a matter for the dog. When you own a dog
there is an option to dress it up in a trench coat
or checked sweater, or let it get wet and shiver.
There is an option to towel dry it roughly, or gently
or let it dry off by an open fire, or shut it outside
for fear of sullying soft furnishings. When you talk
to a dog, there is an option of the usual commands:
Sit. Beg. Roll over. Heel. Or there is an option
to confide all your secrets and believe its doggy eyes
are full of understanding and forgiveness for every
transgression, and indulgence for each peccadillo.
When you feed a dog, there is an option to choose
dry food for its temperamental stomach, or cook it
a rare steak, or sneak it titbits from the table.
If the dog is sick, there is an option to take it to the vet
or wait and see what happens, or there is an option
of driving a six-inch nail into its head and burying it
in a shallow grave for a passing walker to discover
when she hears whimpering. When you develop
a prototype for a breast implant there is an option
to implant one into a dog called Esmerelda, before
implanting Timmie Jean Lindsey, a factory worker
from Texas with six children, who asked you to remove
only the tattoo of roses which bloomed across her breasts.
When you desire another dog, there is an option
to breed dogs incapable of giving birth naturally

because their heads are disproportionately large.
When the day comes, as it must, and the dog escapes
and a vet is nowhere near, the whelping bitch
will have one option: to push.

The Dogs of Pénestin

Argos[1], Hound[2], Banga[3], Lassie[4],
Son-of-George[5], Bear[6], Snowy[7],

Fang[8], Gyp[9], Old Yeller[10], Toto[11],
Böwser vön Überdog[12], Sorry-oo[13],

Cadpig, Lucky, Roly Poly, Patch[14],
Pearl the Wonder Dog[15], Ponch[16],

Crab[17], Frank the Pug[18], Skulker[19],
Bull's-eye[20], K9[21], John Joiner[22],

Prince Amir of Kinjan[23], Wellington[24],
Hong Kong Phooey[25], Gai-Luron[26],

Sirius[27],
Cerebrus[28].

---

1   Waits by the gate for his mistress, in Syria with
Médecins Sans Frontières.

2   Destroyed for leaving gigantic, muddy footprints.

3   His master is a pilates instructor, partial to a
Margarita Cocktail.

4   Rescued a young boy from the sea at Loscolo.

5   Sheep worrier, hated by Brécean farmer, Gabriele
Chêne.

6   Chocolate Labrador belonging to Luka who also
has a bear called Dog.

7   An adventurous wire-fox terrier regularly walked by a failed abstract artist.

8   Belongs to the seven-foot-six gamekeeper of Le Lesté.

9   Trots at the heels of his carpenter master.

10 Enjoys wild boar hunts with Travis Manteaux.

11 Penchant for chewing his mistress's red slippers.

12 A vicious bulldog; detests the llamas from Cirque Medrano.

13 Howls at the moon and dreams of his wolf brothers in Brocéliande.

14 Puppies owned by Cruella de la Ville, a supporter of Marine Le Pen.

15 German Shorthaired Pointer, a couch potato pooch.

16 Appears to live in some sort of squirrel universe.

17 Described by his incontinent master as a cruel-hearted cur.

18 Owned by a policeman who claims he can talk.

19 Huge, purple tongue hangs half a foot out of his mouth.

20 A white shaggy dog, with his face scratched and torn in twenty different places.

21 Bark has a metallic ring. His master, Dr. Qui, collects watches.

22 Saved a kitten from being eaten by two giant rats.

23 Afghan Hound puppy that makes a mess on the cliff paths.

24 Poodle involved in a gardening accident.

25 Belongs to a mild-mannered janitor who dabbles in martial arts.

26 Melancholic Basset Hound from the same litter as Droopy.

27 Heavenly dog worshipped by all the other dogs of Pénestin.

28 No-one who enters his property, Enfer, is seen coming out alive.

Anonymous
after the New Yorker cartoon by Peter Steiner, 1993

On the internet, nobody knew I was a dog,
how I'd raise my hind-leg to piss, bark
viciously at cats on my anonymous blog.

O trolls, those dog days were a lark.
I, Sirius, outshone all in the Canis Major,
blew my master's whistle in his park.

Bitch! he yelled. *Track and cage her.*
Failed to guess at my dog's bollocks,
as I buried my bone-to-pick deeper

in the Darknet where encryption locks.
Once bitten, twice bitcoin:
a silken road to Anything Stocked.

Second lifer, don't whimper - feign
identities. Dangle spam bait, flog
lives as authorities neuter the anodyne.

Only saps are hacked as they iSlog.
On the internet, nobody knows I am a dog.

A Chorus of Jacks in 13 Texts

after Porphyria

U R t% BUTful 4 yor Lyf 2 nd happily, t% BUTful 4 a closing shot of
    yor fAc :-)
in2 a soapy sunset

We knew he'd b a cad, wear u lIk arm candy, reveal intimacies Ovr
    cards f he c%d plA
NEthing mo sophisticated thN >@< Crush

He mA L%k lIk a Victorian gentleman, w Hs moustache & side-
    burns, bt he's a digital darling,
kEpn Hs connections OpN

U wer born out of era. aL yor letters shud b RitN on violet paper,
    scented w
violet water, sealed w a violet :-*

insted U R forced 2 sext DIS vile man, endure Hs violent demands 4
    <) & beer,
Hs insistence dat tap H2O iz BetA 2 bathe n thN bubLE

We hav Hs number, we hav aL Hs on9 accounts hacked. d 3:o) he met
Bhind yor beautifully-boned bak iz not evN an on9 comment, a
    Facebook Like, retweet,
not evN hEr

Don't wori we wud not harm a hair on yor hed cuz U L%k aftR yor
    hair, & she didn't.
It wz tied bak w a rubR band, & itz casualness wz unbearable

2 tink how he wound dat rat tail rownd Hs fingers wen dey kissed,

whIl U sat aloN by d window,
yor tresses holdN d moon's gleam

2 tink dat makes us cry & so she had 2 cry too, 2 knO how much it
    hrtz 2 luv U lIk we do

4giv us 4 bn soppy, bt U mAk us sentimental, mAk us txt things we
    shouldn't,
mAk us flame, mAk us troll

Really, it's yor fault. f it wz not 4 yor yeLo hair, yor smooth white
    sholdR bare,
we wud not hav 2 luv U lIk we do, not hav 2 foLow U on Instagram

foLow U om, let ourselves in2 yor basement w d key code texted 2 d
    cad, hu won't b comin,
won't eva b comin anywhere eva agen

W8 2 presnt U w aL her hair n 1 lng yeLo string az a token of our
    tragic luv

Clutch

Slapped away his ovum-filching fingers

I am not cuckoo
I keep my eggs about me
clutched and warm-nested

Climbed a branch and brooded

Deciduous girls
dropping eggs like leaves
yolking the dark earth

Eggs eyed-up and guarded

A golden goose kept
by a medical giant
lays golden gametes

In the Forest of Anagram, a warning: Fire is Rife!

A fibrous nest burns
thin twigs up in smoke
as the moss smoulders

*Eggers, oologists, experts plan raids in the spring
On Holderness and beyond*

How much more thieving?
Peacock eyes watch eggs blown through
in a begging bowl

Aphid Reproduction as Unpunctuated White Noise

.

a full stop is an aphid not a comma nor an embryo
an aphid is a full stop is a nymph not a womb holding
a comma nor a question mark asks nothing of a slash
or a backslash bulges with parentheses bears
afterthought after afterthought as a full stop
parthenogenetic filled with full stops without
stopping without comma without pausing full stop
after full stop never comma not a comma until
all the space is taken with full stop upon full stop
not a comma and a full stop develops wings flies off

!

an exclamation mark is an aphid on the wing not a
full stop not a comma nor an embryo an aphid is
an exclamation mark not a womb holding a comma
nor a question mark asks nothing of a slash or a
backslash bulges with parentheses bears afterthought
after afterthought as a full stop parthenogenetic
not an exclamation mark not a comma but a full stop
filled with exclamation marks filled with full stops
bears exclamation marks filled with full stops
until summer heat has happened and love is in the air

an aphid is a male on the wing not a full stop
is an exclamation mark and an aphid is a female
on the wing not a full stop is an exclamation mark
gives birth to a full stop without wings mates
with an exclamation mark and lays a full stop
a full stop is an egg not an aphid but an egg
and the egg it is dormant is a full stop not a pause
not a comma nor an embryo but a full stop in the winter
without wings an egg is a full stop until spring
and it hatches a full stop is an aphid not a full stop

VI.

Legend

BASEMENT EXCAVATION[1]

1   I had a vision, and it was inward,
downward if you like, deeper than my thoughts
and it stretched from my tax avoidance to
Derinkuyu. And it told me, Dig, Dig,
Dig. I am no Diogenes sleeping
in a ceramic jar. But the earth, O
the dirt, dirt of sweet evacuation.
In my bowels, I yearn for emptying out
the centre of the earth in worm castings
to create space for a vaulted vacuum.
Have you seen my wish list, my architect
of gloom? Stalactites of diamonds hanging
over gold tiles Mammon and Mammon laid.
Stalagmites of Ferraris revving up
columns of static speed. I will not stop,
cannot be blocked: bathrooms, ballroom, gunroom.
Shit, shimmy, shoot. May I invite you to
a pre-screening of Pandemonium?
All the devils star. Play Persephone!
Come, shuck oysters, fork snails, drown ortolans
in vats of Armagnac and crunch on bones,
spit out feet, no napkin to cover eyes –
here there is no shame. Here we come to purge.

Colchester Native

Oysters shucked. Poor man's beef discarded
down guts and out again to sea. Shells salvaged.
Here, concentrated behind wire mesh, hard stuffing
for this upholstered seat placed for musing
on the river Colne. Quantities shipped on
circuitous routes to sate Elizabethan London.
The centre sucking resources in greedy gulps.
Local beds, and locals lay wasted in leaner times.
What now? Lean back on shells, characteristically
flat, the flesh enjoyed by Romans firm and salty,
a wet dream of these parts. Orgiastic oysters,
slipping down, coming up, their stockmarket fortunes,
bivalve biology, always two sides to prize apart:
rich & poor, insider & outsider. Pearly junkets
or gritty chronicles? Filter feeders, take it all in and sift
through for dignitaries at the annual Oyster Feast
by invitation only since Saint Dennis held his fair.
Left out in the cold, sit back, digest world wars
and viruses, how oyster numbers could not atone:
oistre, ostreum, ostreon. Osteon, so close to bone.

And I Have Seen

And I have seen the river aflame
        stalking the air like a tiger
And I have seen it flash orange and black
And I have known the river bed crack
And I have known blackside dace die in Kentucky
And I have heard our leaders speak
        in bubbles of methane
And I have heard that people foresake
        their claim to land for the promise of baubles
And I have feared of troubles
        water that runs black, oranges that grow in lungs
        oranges that grow black, troubles that run in water
And I have feared of lungs
        their claim to people for the promise of land
And I have heard that leaders foresake
        in baubles of methane
And I have heard our bubbles speak
And I have known blackside dace die in the river bed
And I have known Kentucky crack
And I have seen it flash orange and black
        stalking the air like a tiger
And I have seen the river aflame

What Though the Field Be Lost?

All is not lost; hedge, mere memory of a jade belt
hitching up honeysuckle, sentiment of Eve's blighted breast.
Who would crave the stain of a thorn'd Blackberry welt,

envy a nutshell crown, save some dull Cromwell dressed
in country colours? Let us not regret the canker
of an apple tree when below roots, blasted earth is blessed

with ribs of gold. Rush, shovel-ready to plough and pilfer
rights in anthill strongholds. The prick of a whore's thorn,
berry bright globules, seeded with cyanide that spur

us onto bulldozer battle against acres of banal corn.
Speculate a spectacle of grey on grey crop rising
in concrete mist, reliquary for rooks, a Babel born

as voices clamour for profit. Our caw of capital surmising
the fox ungloved, all weed a bind, each skin a pelt.
A buildable plot to crush green and wooden moralising.

When finance is the field in which environment knelt –
all is not lost; hedge joins fund. Our treasury, a jaded belt.

Apple Quartet

i. Jaune de Metz

Repeat *If you love me, pop and fly. If you hate me,*
burn and die, and think of your amour as you cast
a pip in the fire. At my ripe age, I look on wildings

with a jaundiced eye. Once skin was golden
like the future. Fortune is a liar. He the scion
of a rich family, I from strong stock. Such notions

of choice; in the hearth, a pip scorched desire. No ladders
to reach an apple hanging like a heart in hock. I grafted,
kept close to the earth, was nothing to birdsong,

good breeding in every branch to which pickers
would flock. My crown not high enough for sheep
to graze beneath, among village gossip, wisdom of

soil and season, gatherings to celebrate harvest
with cider and song. *Old apple tree we wassail thee*
superseded by reason. Longing for lanterns, ribbons

to tie around limbs betrayed by the aphid's
white ruff of treason. What auguries in peel
can the earth descry? *If you hate me, burn and die.*

ii. The Apple Machine

Where worms, roots and fingers
mesh, the future is buried in an apple
machine: Redlove sliced

for ruddy flesh. No dwarfing rootstock
helped the queen control the apple
that blessed the bough. A poisoned mind

finds time to dream. Dwarfs mined mountains
for rubies – now *Malling 9* is paradise
preserved. We scatter before we plough,

discard the fruit that isn't curved
to mimic the perfect orb of the sun;
a diamond bite cosmetically preferred

by queens, kings, everyone. A tooth
puller in a souk in Marrakesh wields
pliers to pluck what fireblight

has undone. Like a princess we sleep
in the machine's crèche where worms,
roots and fingers mesh.

iii. Here, Apple Tree

Here, branches are stark against white
sky, their bronchial diagram a lesson in
breath. A snared plastic bag puffs with

effort to fly free of some small death,
empty of exotic fruit carried
from shelves, the carrier holds its own

trashed shibboleth. Here, custom rots slower
than our apple selves, rosy at the
buffet, all you can eat for the price of burst

buttons, girdles, belts loosening
at the heart's abnormal beat to a defibrillation
rhythm, a wassail haunting the wind

in clamour for retreat from acres
of sterilised soil. Half-recalled, *If you hate
me burn and die,* blown fireblight,

an orange sun's broil. On the out breath,
If you love me, pop and fly. Here,
branches are white against stark sky.

iv. A is for Apple

Abbot's Early, Ashmead's Kernel, Autumn Pearmain
Barchard's Seedling, Billy Down Pippin, Bloody Butcher
Cap of Liberty, Carswell's Honeydew, Cummy Norman

Doctor Clifford, Dog's Snout, Duke of Devonshire
Early Bower, Easter Orange, Eccleston Pippin
Fair Maid of Taunton, Falstaff, Forest Styre

George Carpenter, Gillyflower of Gloucester, Gin
Hall Door, Hangydown, Hope Cottage Seedling
Improved Woodbine, Irish Peach, Iron Pin

Jackets and Waistcoats, Jo Jo's Delight, Jordan's Weeping
Keed's Cottage, Kernel Underleaf, Kingston Black
Leathercoat Russet, Lemon Queen, Lucombe's Seedling

Macfree, Marston Scarlett Wonder, Merton Prolific
Nancy Jackson, Netherton Late Blower, Neverblight
Oaken Pippin, Old Cornish Cooker, Onion Redstreak

Painted Summer Pippin, Palmer's Rosey, Pam's Delight
Quarren Dow, Quarry, Queen Caroline
Racky Down, Radford Beauty, Rathe Ripe

Slack-ma-Girdle, Snell's Glass Apple, Sops-in-Wine
The Rattler, Tinsely Quince, Tower of Glamis
Underwood Pippin, Upright French, Upton Pyne

Vagnon Archer, Valentine, Vallis
Wardington Seedling, Warrior, Wealthy
Excel Jonagold, Excelsior, Exeter Cross

Yarlington Mill, Ye Old Peasgood, Yellow Ingestrie
Yeovil Sour, Yorkshire Aromatic, Zari.

VII.

Neatline

Fragmentation: Top Ten Objects, Grant Museum of Zoology

i. Quagga

One of only seven
quagga skeletons
zebra, South African
fewer stripes than
the last died in Amsterdam
rumours and examination
donkey, one specimen

ii. Thylacines

Tigers, Tasmanian
marsupials, adaptation
convergent evolution
1936, hunted to extinction
politics delayed action
Wilf Batty killed last wild specimen
head and paws removed during dissection

iii. Dodo Bones

Icons of extinction
disappeared by 1861
related to pigeon
Mauritius, Indian Ocean
cats and pigs brought by humans
man realised his actions
mock-up dodos in collections

iv. Giant Deer

From Siberia to Ireland
years ago, seven thousand
antlers shed, weighing up to 45 kilograms
cold and warm transitions
reached Europe, humans
disappeared populations
Elkie spotted in hotel in Ireland

v. Blaschka Glass Models of Invertebrates

Glass sea cucumbers in collection
jellyfish, anemone, cephalopod specimens
Leopold, Rudolph, long line of Czech artisans
jewellers working in Dresden
1888 models accession
Blaschkas' skills died with them
display of glass models, out of fashion

vi. The Micrarium

displaying 2,323 tiniest specimens
big animals in most museums
converted an old office/storeroom
slides from zoologists R.B. Freeman
J.P. Hill, G.H. Fowler, D.M.S. Watson
95% of known animal species smaller than
your thumb

vii. Jar of Moles

Eighteen moles, preservation
jar efficient storage: one reason
intended for dissection
inhabit deciduous woodland
grassland, farmland
talpa europaea, mole European
found in Russia and Britain

viii. The Brain Collection

Majority come from
The Gordon Museum Brain Collection
originally from Kings' School of Medicine
comparative anatomy collection
tiger cub's, domestic dog's brain
tiny label stapled to each section
except for a single turtle, mammals' brains

ix. African Rock Python Skeleton

Arrived from London Zoo a whole specimen
skin in poor condition
remove the flesh, prepare the skeleton
documented as green anaconda in collection
suggest from photos snake in question
not an anaconda: along their backs spotted pattern
looks like an African rock python

x. *The Negus Collection of Bisected Heads*

Chimp, wallaby, sloth, seal, pangolin
lemur, wolf fish, shrew in collection
Negus specimens at Royal College of Surgeons
Negus worked on anatomy of larynx in animals and humans
may remind you of work of artist Damien
cut in two to display nose and throat structure, brain
beautifully presented specimens

Let Them Leave Language to Their Lonely Betters

after W. H. Auden's 'Their Lonely Betters'

This is not a poem about a robin or a blackbird
for although I love birdsong, I've never heard
a song I can say for certain came from that bush
having looked quick enough to identify a thrush.

Their names are withheld from their songs
which fly freely about an ear that no longer longs
to sort out this chirrup from that trill
so I can distinguish this beak from that bill.

This muddle of medley is an anthem of all
and no proper name can answer each call
which remains unrecorded in its own shade,
undetonated by a signifier's semantic grenade.

Let them leave language to this lonely better
who has struggled too long with nomenclature;
let me sing my own song, and hear what I can,
it will sound how it is – of robin, or of man.

A Sudden Wind

The sprig, rigged by the wind with nerve endings,
frights as a blackbird takes flight *suddenly* –
a word the poet notes was the poet's favourite,
now dumb on the un-thumbed page, as fire rages
in the library, devouring paper. A downdraught
dislodges a bird trapped in the flue; falling
suddenly on the charcoaled heap: dried twigs,
orange pips, an old nest. Suddenly's animus
not an ill wind; a bellow for life – bellows filling
with rage at an age of snuffed lights,
the breath rattle in the throat, and not a candle
held, but a blackbird suddenly may chase a kite.

A Heart Pumps in Service

If I were to ask you to take the heat out of your heart,
you would be left with *r*, Law of Laplace,
where *r* is the radius, which has something
to do with blood flow and the relationship
between pressure and tension within a sphere.

Friend, I know your heart hurts,
burns less fiercely than it did before,
but my orange material mouth,
tapestry tongue are flammable,
which is why I persist with the physics of this.

If I were to ask you to take the art out of your heart,
you would be left with *he*, that male one
who is neither speaker nor hearer,
but dominates generic conversation –
listens out to block, if *she* tries to interpose.

Friend, I know your heart hurts,
pumps less easily than it did before,
but my pink material mouth,
tapestry tongue are manufactured,
which is why I persist with the politics of this.

If I were to ask you to take the ear out of your heart,
you would be left with *h-t*, short for handheld transceiver
which sounds like a heart in hand,
originally intended for military use.
only letting one lub-DUB talk at a time.

Friend, I know your heart hurts,
beats less loudly than it did before,
but my moth-eaten material mouth,
tapestry tongue are cloth-eared,
which is why I persist with the silence of this.

Notes

Corona/Cuts: this crown of sonnets uses lines and images from John Donne's 'A Valediction: Forbidding Mourning'; 'A Valediction of Weeping'; 'At the round earth's imagin'd corners, blow'; The good-morrow'; 'Batter my heart, three person'd God...'; and 'Aire and Angels'.

Written in 1939, Joaquín Rodrigo's 'Concierto de Aranjuez' was inspired by the gardens at Palacio Real de Aranjuez. The second movement is a response to the miscarriage of his first child.

Antes muerto que mudado (sooner dead than changed) is the Spanish inscription engraved on the Portrait of John Donne, aged 18 in the second edition of his Poems, printed in 1635 and then again in 1639, and held by the British Library

The reasons given by teenage boys for carrying knives are taken from interviews in the *Guardian* newspaper and BBC news reports.

Knife Angel is a sculpture made by Alfie Bradley with knives donated by police forces around the country at the British Ironworks Centre at Oswestry, Shropshire.

Acknowledgements

A big thank you to the editors of the magazines where some of these poems first appeared. I know the work involved in editing, so thanks to my Magma co-editors, Susannah Hart (Conversation Issue) and Raymond Antrobus (Deaf Issue) and to all the Magma team, past and present.

Thank you to the Torriano Meeting House, the welcome of Sunday evenings' open floor spots, and the Thursday Poetry Group.

Thank you to my wonderful poetry tutor, Jane Draycott, at Lancaster University, and to my fellow students for their help, friendship and support.

Thank you to Michael Schmidt and Andrew Latimer for their editorial guidance and to all the Carcanet team for their help during the process of putting this book together and beyond. Thank you to Jim, Lottie, Dane, Linda, Jimmy, Simon, Nyra and Emma for being there.

'Aubade for an Artist' was published in *Under the Radar*, Summer 2016

'Life Model' was published in *Long Poem Magazine*, Issue 11

'Six Perspectives on Lilian Kjærulff' was published in *Ambit*, Issue 215; and by *And Other Poems*

'A&E' was published in *The Spectator*

'Death Certificate, Burnt Oak' was published in the anthology *The Book of Love and Loss*; and by *Culture Matters*

'The Shadow Cast' was published in *Ambit*, Issue 220

'Ø' was published in *The Interpreter's House*, #56

'This is not a Road Trip' was published in *South Bank Poetry*, issue 28

'A Desultory Day' was published in *The Rialto*, Issue 85

'Trailing Spouse' was published in *Ambit*, Issue, 229

'Wavering' was published in *Magma*, Issue 61

'Out of Order' was part of the winning submission to Lancaster
University's open competition on Reading (MA Category)

'Philip Levine's Good Ear' was published by *Antiphon*, Issue 20

'Herring Loss' was published by *Antiphon*, Issue 17; and the
anthology *Stairs and Whispers: D/Deaf and Disabled Poets Write
Back* (Nine Arches Press)

'Best Seat in the House' was published in the anthology *Stairs
and Whispers: D/Deaf and Disabled Poets Write Back* (Nine
Arches Press)

'A Map Towards Fluency' was published in *Ambit*, Issue 231

'Obelus' was published in the anthology *Asterism* (Laudanum)

'Cuddles are Drying up Like the Sun in a Data Lake' was
published in *Tears in the Fence*, Issue 65

'Clavicle Snaps' was published in *Ambit*, Issue 229

'Saltatorium' was published in *Brittle Star*, Issue 41

'Twenty Grains, One Scruple' and 'Playing Dog' were published
in *Fenland Reed*, Issue 6

'The Dogs of Pénestin' was on the longlist for the 2016 National
Poetry Competition

'Anonymous' was published in *Prole*, Issue 18

'A Chorus of Jacks in 13 Texts' was published in *Tears in the
Fence*, Issue 65

'Clutch' was published in *Finished Creatures*, Issue 1

'Polar Observations with Anagram Shadows' was published in
Brittle Star, Issue 41

'And I Have Seen' was published in *The Morning Star*

'Apple Quartet' was published in *PN Review*, 232, Volume 43
Number 2, November-December 2016

'A Sudden Wind' was published in *New Walk Magazine*, Issue 10

Some of the poems also previously appeared in *New Poetries VII*
(Carcanet, 2018) and *Philip Levine's Good Ear* (Stonewood
Press, 2018)